THE 30-DAY

NO SPEND CHALLENGE

GUIDE

TABLE OF CONTENTS

INTRODUCTION

Life comes with so many challenges that put us under pressure. Most of these challenges arise because we need to make ends meet; when we can't meet our needs, it is a heavy weight on us. It clutters the mind, places a burden on your mental health, stress you out.
In a bid to take care of the debt or save for a particular purpose we can go into more debt and this is more burdensome.

This book shows a different way to handle your finances.

You will learn how to

- Declutter and organize your mind: when your mind is organized, you make sound financial decisions.

- Live a stress-free life

- Live a minimalist lifestyle

- Make a budget and prioritize your expenses

- Simplify your life

- Spend less

- And learn other important spending tips

Your finances will never remain the same when you are done reading the book.

CHAPTER ONE
DE-CLUTTER AND ORGANIZE YOUR MIND

Whatever thought you have about money comes first from your mind. This is why I am taking out this chapter to talk about the mind and put it in the right order.

Why is the mind important?

This chapter may seem like one of those chapters but it is essential. This is because the mind is the seat of all actions taken and words said. This is because it acts like a sponge that soaks up information before turning it into knowledge that will lead to the right action.

The mind can run into overdrive and when it is in this state, you can't function properly because it is in a mess. Just like boxes cupboards and even cabinets, our minds can be cluttered; it can be packed and filled with a lot of things so there will be a need for you to tidy it up from time to time. Since the mind is the power house, it needs to be cleared up and organized from time to time; without this you wouldn't be creative, focused or inspired. This will affect the kinds of decisions you will make.

So how can your de-clutter your mind?

1. Make a list of your priorities: when you set your priorities, you are taking sure steps to take your mind back from the clutter which is a way to take charge of your life. You need to first figure out what is important and what is urgent. What is important may not be urgent while what is urgent may be important.

I use the four quadrants of time managements: it's basically 4 quadrants.

- Quadrant 1: Urgent but important

- Quadrant 2: Not urgent and important

- Quadrant 3: Not important but urgent

- Quadrant 4: Not urgent and important.

This quadrant is really helpful. Sometimes I feel like everything has to be done right now so I spend most of my time on the urgent things instead of focusing on the important things. There are times I mix both up. To avoid this, I will give you a hint of what is urgent, not urgent, important and not important.

- Urgent and important: These activities are what I refer to as life and death situations. They are emergencies and crisis that arise.

- Not urgent and important: These are activities that require you to plan ahead; they help you to prepare for crisis and they help you improve and become better. This may include studying or getting informed.

- Not important but urgent: these activities are what make you busy. They can wait for a while and take the back seat while you move on to other important things.

- Not important and not urgent: these activities usually waste your time. You can live for 24 hours without doing them. For me, social media and fiddling with my phone takes the bulk of the not important and not urgent things I do.

After categorizing all your activities into the 4 quadrants, you need to create a plan that can help you meet up with all your plans.

Sometimes your priorities can change and grow so make sure your list of priorities and goals are flexible enough to accommodate change.

2. Journaling is a must: What some people don't understand is that journaling is therapeutic. When you keep a journal, you help your mind to set itself in order and prepare for all the activities ahead. When you write out your thoughts, you take away negative thoughts and you can focus on the important stuff. This will make your mind free to

focus on other important things and you will notice that you wouldn't easily get stressed. Some people feel that they have to be a writing pro to be able to start journaling. This is all together wrong and it is not an excuse. You don't have to be the world's best writer to start journaling; you can begin by writing out your points and you can develop the points when you feel that you have the right words to express yourself. Don't forget it is your journal so there is no one going to read it except you. Don't put any pressure to be a perfect writer.

3. Let go of the negatives: you need to learn how to accept your weakness and strengths in the same manner; by this I mean don't let your weaknesses weigh you down and your strengths should also

not be a reason for you to be proud. Work on your weakness and don't let them draw you back. If it draws you back then it will clutter your mind. When you let go of the negative thoughts, worries and fears, you will be able to de-clutter your mind and relieve it of stress which is what will help you make good decisions. Whenever you think of something negative, replace it with the positives.

4. Stop multi-tasking: I know someone might be thinking I'm crazy by making this statement but trust me when I say multi-tasking makes you counter-productive. This is because you can get side tracked into so many things at once. By doing 4 things at once, you will only be able to give 25% in one activity, 15% in another activity, 50% in

another and 10% in another. Besides, multi-tasking will take more of your time on one activity which is more time than you will spend if you focus on only one activity. You get more stressed and give room for clutter to get into your mind when you multi-task. Focus on one single task and stick with it. Don't forget the time management quadrant, use that to focus on the activities you want to do.

5. Take time to practice breathing exercises: sit down, relax and breathe in. Hold your breath for 10 seconds and release it slowly. Do it 3 times and examine how you feel. I'm sure you will feel great afterwards. Deep breath is an awesome means to clear clutter in the mind. It takes your mind off

worries, makes you feel good and makes you calm deep within. If your blood pressure is high, it helps to reduce it and makes your mind relax at the same time. By consistently carrying out breathing exercises you can boost your immune system and concentrate better.

6. Take out the clutter in your work area: when you have a messy or totally clutter work area, you are bound to get frustrated and this will waste your time. Organize your work table and your work area. For some people who work on their laptops, you may need to clear your desktop. Arrange your documents in folders so it doesn't look to messy or cluttered. This will help you to do away with unimportant stuff and focus on the important ones.

7. Be decisive with your decisions: sometimes clutter comes as a result of delay in making decisions. I understand that you may need to take your time when you are making some decisions and it can clutter your mind. To avoid this, write out your thoughts on every decision. Avoid procrastinating and be swifter in making your decisions. This is why the next point is important.

8. Get role models: you need role models who can motivate and influence you positively. When you have challenges that clutter your mind, you can share it with them and get headway whenever you are confused. This is also a way to release the pent-up emotions in you. They can help you see clearly and better. You will also get a creative solution to

any challenge so that you can make better decisions.

9. Reduce the quantity of media information you consume: you may not know it but the media especially social media takes a toll on your mental health. Research has shown that it causes anxiety, stress, clog your mind and other mental health challenges. Many people on social media are living a fake lifestyle so it may be fool hardy to take up all you see as the whole truth and nothing but the truth. Moreover, by limiting the time you spend on social media and the information you receive from there you can make better decisions without the pressures that come with social media use. When taking up content from the media, be selective with

the kind of information you take and only use reliable sites.

10.   Take out time to pamper yourself: give yourself occasional breaks. You need it! Your mind needs to relax and unwind to make sound financial decisions. Relax with your friends, go to the beach or the spa and unwind. You can also read a book, take a long walk and visit a place with good scenery of nature. Your mind will thank you for this.

Now that you understand how to de-clutter your mind, you can't just leave it that way. If you do, it will be the same thing as getting a bank account and not getting your account details which means you can't use your account. You need to know how to organize your mind.

So how do you organize your mind?

According to research, each person has more than 50,000 different thoughts in a day. If your mind is really active or you do more of mental tasks than physical task then you can have between 70,000 -100,000 thoughts in a day.

Now this fact is huge; you have so many thoughts running through your mind and many of these thoughts run at the same time breaking into your thoughts, distracting you and making you disorganized if you give it the power. The more you let the thoughts run around, the more the thoughts control you. If you don't organize your mind you have a higher chance of having a non-productive day.

With an organized mind, you will be able to flow in the right direction. This means that you will be balanced and you can do your tasks without any form of distraction. You will be able to think properly and work at the peak of productivity.

Here are a few steps to help you organize your mind, find balance and to also be productive.

Understand the challenge you can take and engage it: After de-cluttering your mind, it is easy to get lost in the midst of the many creative thoughts running through the mind especially if the task on your plate is extremely challenging or if it is too simple.

All the mind needs to function effectively is a healthy challenge: this is something that isn't too difficult or demanding that can lead to anxiety or something that is too easy which can lead to boredom. When you pick a task that isn't too simple or challenging, you will boost the effectiveness of your mind and become organized and balanced.

If you are wondering what to do about intrusive thoughts, it's pretty simple to handle. Write them down on notepad or have a sticky note on your table. I prefer a hard copy form of writing; this is because if you use your phone, you have a higher chance of getting distracted.

Be in charge of your emotions: sometimes our feelings want to take control over everything. To give your feelings a leeway is going to be equal to destruction. It is the same thing as buying everything in a fashion store because you have the money and not because you need it. Don't let this happen!

You need to be in control of how you react to everything around you. How does this happen? Pretty simple! Be truthful to yourself. If you are buying a new gadget or a new watch then you need to know why you are indulging yourself to get these things. Is it a luxury or are you buying it as a reaction then you are indulging your emotions and it isn't the right thing to do.

When you can identify your emotions and you understand why you are making your financial decisions in a particular way, you can control it and direct it to make the right decisions that you want. Find the right words to express how you feel so you can demystify the funny feeling. — Journal your emotions -

If you don't balance your emotions it may be extremely challenging to make sound financial decisions and you can make positive financial achievements. Without this, your emotions will cloud your mind and stand in the way of your reasoning.

Eyes on the prize: I can't begin to explain how challenging it is whenever I lose sight on my goals and focus. But I have learnt one thing: to turn back and focus on my goal when I remember. To build your focus you must be able to stay with one activity for at least 20 minutes. Take away everything that can be a distraction. It could be electronic gadgets and mobile devices especially those with games and those that can connect to the internet. You need to face your aim heads-on without distraction.

Take breaks from time to time: for your mind to be organized you need to take time out as a break period. This will enable you to get the best out of every moment.

Set a time period for your tasks: try to finish tasks before taking a break and when you are done with the break then you can move to the next task. This will encourage you to balanced and more organized.

CHAPTER TWO
SIMPLIFY YOUR LIFE AND BECOME A MINIMALIST

I chose to become a minimalist so many years ago and I have never had a cause for regret. I have been enjoying simpler life with no regrets. Over the years, people have asked me the principles I have used to stay debt free, stress free and happy.

The answer is pretty simple; unlike many people, I don't allow my finances to control me. This answer doesn't satisfy everyone because many people tell me financial issues are usually complicated. Whenever I hear that financial issues are complicated, I tell them one thing: Simplify!

To make this easier for you, I have been able to put the principles I have learnt over the years into points that you can follow. These principles worked for me and I believe they will also work for you and give you control over your life.

Reduce the number of bank accounts you have

In case you don't know, you will do well if you only have one savings account and one checking account. If you have many accounts, you can either close them all or merge them all into one. This way you will be able to simplify banking without incurring extra costs or running into loss from servicing the accounts.

You can do this for your retirement accounts. If you have many reduce them and simplify your life and roll all your retirement plans to a self-directed IRA account. This will reduce the bank charges; paper work and you can supervise and manage your retirement assets easily.

Reduce the paperwork to the barest minimum

With many accounts for various financial reasons comes the huge amount of paperwork that follows suit in your house. For me, I didn't have time to read through each one of them but seeing the huge stack of papers cluttered my mind and stressed me. One day I decided to consolidate the accounts and trash all the papers. I felt so relieved that day.

Take out all the paper that isn't useful or totally important. This is because it will clutter your mind and de-simplify your life (which is what we have to avoid). First of all, cut down on your accounts and then your paperwork will reduce and this will reduce your stress in turn.

Stick with a single credit card

If you are someone who is into discounts, promotions or interest rate rewards, I'm sure you may have quite a number of credit cards. The thing about interest rates and rewards is that once all promotional offers or discounts are over, the cards have little or no value.

I advise you to focus on one credit card in case you decide to keep the other cards open to gain credit points. Find out the one single card that offers you more benefits than others and focus on that one card. It is pretty much easier to supervise one card and how you spend with it than to use several cards for payments.

Live debt free

Debt is more than money; it is about your mind, your mental health. Every part of you will get worked up even subconsciously and it makes your life complicated not simplified. You will spend more time servicing debts, paying bills and incurring stress on your mind. The truth is that as you finishing servicing one debt, you will remove one layer of stress and complication from your life.

Staying debt free is not something that happens at the snap of your hand; you need to work towards it by creating a budget and creating a payment plan. When you do this and work towards it then your life will become simpler.

While investing, focus on funds in place of individual stocks

Its more common to find people to invest in individual stocks than to invest in funds because individual stocks is rewarding and fun; but many people forget how stressful it can be. This is because you have to take out the time to read and get information about the stocks so you can buy, track it and sell each one. Having as many as the finger on one hand can be overwhelming because it is a job on its own.

You can live free from all the stress that comes from investing in individual funds by focusing your investment in mutual funds or by exchanging traded funds. While investment in individual stocks have a long process for tax related documentation, investing in funds is easier when it is time to file for tax return.

Opt for cash: pay cash as much as you can

This sounds like something from the 19th century but the fact remains that paying with cash has its own benefits. It means you wouldn't need receipts and you wouldn't need to track your expense which is what happens when you use your credit or debit card. You don't need to look back when you pay with cash.

You can use your credit card when you are buying things in large quantity that would guarantee potential refund and buyer protection. Cash is a way to make life simpler, trust me!

Remove wants from your budget; stick with your needs

It's simpler to stick with your needs and not your wants (because you can live without your wants). Subscriptions and services, you rarely use should be crossed out of your budget. When you take them off, you save more money and this simplifies your life. When you have fewer bills to pay, you will see that your life is simpler.

Avoid writing a long list of goals

When you have a long list of goals, you focus on how to make all of them work at once. This has a disadvantage; you stretch yourself into too many things at once and you cannot be effective in everything at once. It's best you limit the number of goals you have and pour yourself into. This way you can maximize your strength for each one. This will reduce distraction, clutter and confusion.

You can focus on one or two goals in a month, focus on them and pursue them like that's the last thing you will ever do. You will be able to accomplish them in a matter of time so you can move on to the next goal as quickly as possible.

It's better to rent a home than to own one

Owning a home is what we have always known to be the best and that's what financial experts have always preached. But no one talks about the huge cost of running a house and responsibilities that are linked to owning a home. When you compare this to the responsibilities that come with renting a house, you will see that renting a house makes your life simpler. You wouldn't need to worry about maintenance, repairs and other costs; that is the work of the house owner or landlord.

When you rent an apartment, you can pay for your rent monthly and you will only focus on your utility bills; other things are not your concern so you can live a simpler life.

Focus on what generates more income

If you are self-employed, if you own your business or if you are into sales or marketing, then it is more important to focus on what brings more income to you (this also concerns salary earners too). It's not so much about making money, cashing out is more important and it makes your life simpler so this is what you should focus on.

As much as you can, take the administrative responsibilities off your shoulders by passing it to someone else. As a salary earner, think of something you can do that will also generate extra income for you. This is an awesome way to boost your income and simplify your life.

Switch off the TV and spend lesser time on the Internet

We live in an age where information is almost equal to gold or diamonds. This also means there is a chance that you may have information overload as it may lead to noise and mental clutter. There are financial experts both on TV and Internet who have tons of advice on what you can do to boost your finances and you have to go easy on all of this information.

All the information clutter can take you away from the financial simplicity that you desire. This is why you should cut down on the information that comes into your mind and screen out any information that isn't necessary. Focus on information from trusted financial experts and do away with the rest.

If you can make these few changes, then you can be sure that you will simplify your life.

CHAPTER THREE
THE MOST EFFECTIVE ANTI-SPENDING TRICKS

Our impulses can get the best out of us sometimes; you may be walking down the street and you see a grocery store and you suddenly remember one thing you really need to get; you go on but come out with 5 other important things.

That's the drill for some people. The craziest part is that most of the things we think we really need or the things we buy from impulse are usually left in the house to gather dust because contrary to our impulse, we really don't need them. Some people get to sell theirs and some others aren't so lucky.

Here are some tricks to prevent you from spending money impulsively

- Sleep before you spend

When the thought of buying something creeps up in your mind, take the time to go over it by sleeping over it. Chances are that it will no longer feel like it is so important when you wake up the following day.

- Count the cost

When you want to buy anything on impulse, check out what it costs and how long it will take for you to make the money. If you want to buy a shoe that costs $50, find out how long it will take for you to make $50 and ask if it is really worth it. This way you demotivate yourself from buying it.

- Have your debt or savings in view

When you have a budget there is something you are working towards; it could be paying off a debt or trying to save some more. This should be your concern and always think about this before spending.

- Are you leaking money?

Sometimes we have subscriptions to cover (even though we don't use the subs). The best thing you can do is to go through your bank accounts to be sure that you aren't leaking money to a source you don't use or a source you forgot to unsubscribe from. Cancel these subs and you may be surprised that you may get a refund on some of them. Be sure that you really need these subscriptions because some of them are luxuries you can live without.

You can source for cheap alternatives for some of these subs online.

- (Don't spend too much money on food)

Create a budget or a meal plan for your food and follow this plan by buying only the things you wrote on the meal plan. You can add a few snacks to the list and carry them with you wherever you go. This will stop the urge to buy any food on impulse.

- Do go out with your cards

Take only the cash you need. When you go out with your cards, you can fall into the temptation to buy something impulsively. Resist the urge and stick with your plan.

- Resist the urge to go shopping

It's best to stay away from shopping whether you are shopping alone or you are shopping with your friends. It's pretty easy to fall into the temptation of buying something when all the nice things you see are calling for your attention. Shop before the 30-day challenge begins or shop after the challenge.

- Get rid of the old to receive the new

If you are going to buy something, make sure the old one is out. This will prevent your home and your life from clutter. You can try to sell what you had previously so you can make more money for the new stuffs you want to buy.

- Make a list of what you want to buy

You can get carried away when you go to a store; this is why it is better that you write out your list and hold the appropriate cash you need.

- Try shopping online

Some stores sell their groceries online. You can pick the items you want, add it to your cart and pay on delivery. This is a great for shopaholics and people who buy things impulsively. It puts you in check.

- Keep your savings or debt list in your wallet

If you are participating in the 30-day no spend challenge to save money or to pay off your debt, write it on a paper and put this in your wallet. This will put you in check and prevent you from spending money on frivolities.

- Check out websites for free items you need

Instead of spending money on household items such as sofas, baby clothes, toys, coffee machines and other items, you can search online to get these items for free within your neighborhood.

- Your credit card is a debt card

If you are servicing a debt, know that the money you are spending belongs to the bank or credit facility and not you. Until you finish paying up the debt remind yourself that you are not spending your money and work towards paying up the debt.

- Motivate and challenge yourself

When you are working out to pay your debt, you may find out that your mind is open to a lot of things. You can pick up a new hobby such as reading, baking, painting, sewing, or any DIY online. Try out something creative like creating movie nights for yourself at home and try out your own pizza, burger, beer, smoothie or any other drink of your choice. You will see that you will save money this way. Challenge yourself to meet up to your targets and praise yourself when you do this.

- Set up different accounts

It doesn't have to be a bank account; a piggy bank can also do the job. You can use this to gather the money for utilities and when you have the required amount, the rest can be your pocket money. This will encourage you to do this again.

- Create a penny jar

Have a jar where you put your pennies and cents. You will be surprised with the way they come in handy. Nothing is a waste.

- Take your food to work

This is an awesome way to save money. It is also hygienic because you are sure of the content of the food. It will also reduce the temptation to buy things impulsively.

CHAPTER FOUR
CUTTING BACK ON YOUR SPENDING

There are different ways to enjoy your life even if you are engaging in the no spend challenge. You can do all the things you used to do at no cost at all.

Cutting down costs in the home

Here are a few tips to cut down your expenses at home

- Grow your own veggie garden

You can use back of your house or your kitchen to grow your veggies. This is healthy and it will also save you money. Use containers such as an old box to grow the plans. You can grow your own compost to use as a fertilizer.

- Bake

Bake your bread by yourself. If you aren't sure of what you need or how to bake, go online and find out.

- Beer

Start home brewing and brew your own beer. Get details online.

Put old perfume bottles in your drawers: the drawers will pick up the scent and so will your clothes

- Cleaning

Instead of spending a lot of money on cleaning products, try getting white vinegar and use it for your cleaning. To clean your toilet, you can buy any cheap cola. Pour it in the toilet and flush it down after a few minutes. You will notice your toilet is clean and it works more than some expensive toilet cleaners.

- Hiring equipment

If you want to hire equipments, do it during the bank holiday. You will have a free day when you wouldn't be charged for the equipment.

- Washing dishes

When washing dishes use only half a tablet of dishwashing liquid. You can clear the dirt and oil from the dishes before washing them.

- Entertainment

If you need to entertain your friends and family by having a night in with them or putting up something creative for them while you are doing the no spend challenge, there are a few things you can do stay within any budget you have for entertainment

- Nights-in

You can create a night-in and not night out for your family and friends. This is better than going out and spending a lot of money. You can get them to bring a bottle of wine or a snack when coming along.

- Buying foods: search for local restaurants with good but cheap food prices within your neighborhood.

- Holidays: for holidays, camp or swap with your friends in their houses instead of taking a trip and spending money.

- Satellite television: opt for a cheaper free view box instead of subscribing for satellite channels that is expensive and you may not use.

- Beauty and health: Instead of going to the salon to spend so much money there are a few things you can do back on the cost of beauty and health.

- Opt for student night hair cut: student night haircuts in top-notch salons are carried out by students under the supervision of a well-trained hairdresser.

- Opt for sponge or buff puff: use a sponge or buff puff while taking a shower. This will reduce the amount of shower gel you will use. You can use hair conditioner for your legs to soften the skin in place of shaving foam or shaving cream.

- Beauty treatments: for beauty treatments, visit your local beauty college so you can enjoy reduced prices. Many students will be rounding up their training and you can take advantage of their offer or discount.

- Smoking: If you smoke, the best thing you can do for yourself and your health is to quit. Find out groups that can help you stop smoking.

Shopping

It is pretty easy to overspend or buy impulsively when you are in a shop especially when you know that there are discounts or promotions. Here are some few tips and tricks to help you cut costs while you are shopping.

Time your visit to the supermarket: it is best to visit the supermarket late at night because there are more options for reduced prices.

If you are hungry stay away: it isn't a good idea to go shopping when you are hungry. You will find yourself buying expensive junk food that doesn't take the hunger away.

Don't take your kids with you: if you are going shopping, don't take your kids along. Kids always see what they want and they may throw tantrums that force you to buy what they want.

Use the internet: use mails instead of sending text messages or calls if you pass the message via mails.

Use free software: for your PC, opt for free software or open source software. They are economical and they perform the same function in most cases.

Avoid buying gifts: be creative and make something buy yourself as a gift to others.

Get remanufactured ink cartridges: these remanufactured ink cartridges come at half the price of the new and they work well too.

Check out with your family and friends if they have clothes that you can use. Do the same to others.

Save more: you can use the money off coupons and save the money in your piggybank or jar. It doesn't matter if the coupons are online or offline; save it.

Check your tax code: if your tax code is incorrect, you may be paying more tax than you ought you to pay.

Take walk or use a bicycle: this is an exercise and it saves you money spent on gas.

Car repairs: to find out what is wrong with your car, visit the council MOT centre. They don't charge for running a diagnosis.

Use a car share scheme: this is a great way to save money.

CHAPTER FIVE
DEALING WITH FINANCIAL STRESS

Financial stress is a burden and a weight; it isn't something anyone looks forward too. Financial stress is usually as a result of a lot of debt, too little salary or wage, the cost of running a family or raising children, marriage and other creative ideas about running a business that went south or a new business, managing your finance and there are other things that can cause financial stress too.

One worrisome thing about financial stress is that it affects everything; your thoughts, your mind, your relationships with people and every action you take. If you can reduce your financial worry, it will help you to make better financial decisions and make fewer financial decisions.

Here are a few things you can do to reduce financial stress.

1. Have a budget

Before I understood the importance of a budget, I used to think that a budget was only going to add more to your list and give you more stress. This is not true; a budget helps you to put your finances in the right perspective and it reduces your worry over money.

With a budget, you make the right decision on what to spend money on. When you have the right spending plan, you can take care of your immediate needs and also plan towards future goals such as retirement or buying a house or servicing a debt and savings.

When you are budgeting, the most difficult part of budgeting at the beginning is sticking with the budget no matter the challenges that may arise. When you can do this well at the beginning then it will be easier for you and you will stop getting bothered as you continue with it.

Make a monthly budget and flow with it; you can track your expenses and reduce your monthly expenses till you become balanced with your spending.

2. Have money set aside for emergencies

Remember when we were talking about urgent and important quadrant, we talked about crisis and emergencies, you need to set funds aside for this purpose. An unplanned health challenge or a car repair can be really expensive and stressful; you need to stay free from stress for you to be financially balanced.

There's nothing like having an emergency money set aside as part of your budget. You know the good side to saving this money for emergencies? If there are no emergencies, then the money is saved for a better purpose or when emergencies arise. If you can, I advise that you save up to $1,000 in your bank account for emergencies.

You don't have to start with something really big like $100 or $500; you can start with piggy bank savings such as $1 or $10 daily or even $50 weekly. Have a target amount that you set aside for emergencies every month but you can start saving up for it weekly.

To raise funds for this, I also advise that you walk around your house and search for items that are good but you don't use. Sell them to get cash and you will be impressed at how it makes you live a stress-free life.

3. Get help

If creating your budget is too much stress for you or if you can't seem to get a hang on spending even though you have tried your best, then you should seek for help. Don't be ashamed or shy to ask for help; it is simply a way to take the stress off you and give you a better perspective.

You can opt for classes on investment, spending, budgeting, savings, money management and other important personal financial aspects so you can gain the right knowledge to take the right steps to help you make sound financial decisions. You can employ the services of a financial planner.

With a financial planner, you will be able to make proper plans for investment and long-term saving options. This will see you through the future especially if you are considering how to plan for retirement.

Getting a financial planner or taking classes and seeking help is to encourage you and for you to know that you aren't alone when you see those challenges. Sometimes it may be a good idea to speak with a counselor who specializes in credit counseling service. This way you can restructure your debt and think of a better way to manage your creditors.

Another good thing about speaking with someone is that you become accountable and the person can inform you on steps that will determine your progress. You can do this with a friend or a counselor but a class or a support group is a better way to ensure that you are accountable.

For me, the fact that I was to give someone an account of my savings and the spending It did make me cut off all impulsive buying and unnecessary items which was a good thing; that was how I learned how to save more and stop all impulsive spending and buying.

4. Focus on what you can change

Whenever people have financial challenges, it is usually a combination of challenges; it might be a challenge with debt or savings or income or a combination of all of these.

Sometimes the major challenge behind all of this might be your income: you may not make enough money to cover all your bills. If this is your challenge then you need to decide what you can change and what you have to manage.

This is how you go about it: go back to your budget and go through all that you have written there; strike out the things you can live without and think of what you can add to make you to change the situation. This could mean picking up an extra job or going to school so you can be qualified for a better job.

If the major challenge is with an addiction such as a shopping addiction or a spending problem you can join a support group such as Shopaholics Anonymous or other groups that can help you with this.

When you have a plan to handle your challenge and you stay committed to it, then you will notice that your stress level will reduce significantly (and our aim is to live stress-free).

One thing I noticed is that we mix up our needs and our wants. We think our wants are the same thing as our needs and we tell ourselves that we can live without them. There is a difference; you can write out all your needs and honestly strike out the things you can live without for weeks or days.

This might be really difficult at the beginning but you need to have a picture of your overall goal so that you can progress even when you feel frustrated (trust me you will).

Sometimes you might have a relapse in your spending or other challenges you may have. This is not a reason to quit; go easy on yourself and continue with your financial goals after you acknowledge the mistake. Always stick with your budget and find something to help you relax when you feel overwhelmed.

5. Look on the bright side daily

I know someone might say 'Who cares? I am in a financial mess already!' Life comes with its own mess and each person has a slice from it. The idea is to know how to handle this mess in the right way so you live stress-free and feel overwhelmed at the end of the day.

You need to keep journaling about your financial journey. Talk about the highlights and challenges so that when you feel sad or overwhelmed or angry or depressed, you can look at the progress you've made. Just looking at the positive angle is strong enough to cut down your stress and de-clutter your mind.

If you can you can try to find some healthy outlets that are free online; you can also try exercising or taking long walks as these also improve the mood and you will be able to keep your eyes on the goal. This way you will be able to take your eyes off the stress, worry and anxiety that may arise.

CHAPTER SIX
THE NO SPEND CHALLENGE

Now we are in the main point of this book. As a finance coach and counselor, people walk up to me and ask questions such as "Is it possible to take up a no spend challenge? Or how realistic is a no spend challenge? Or 'Is a budget the same thing as the no spend challenge? and many other similar questions.

Let me just say this: the no spend challenge isn't the same thing as your budget. Just as you have a budget, you should also take up the no spend challenge.

There are different types of no spend challenge, this gives you the option from which you can choose the best no spend challenge that suits your finances.

The main aim of the no spend challenge is to cut down on your spending by taking away the unimportant stuff from your budget. Even though the budget is helping you to see your needs and wants and non-essentials, the no spend challenge will help you amplify the unimportant things so you can chop it off totally.

What you should know about the no spend challenge

The no spend challenge is a period that you choose (which could be a few days, one week, a few weeks, or a month) to net spend any money at all. We are working towards a 30-day no spend challenge.

The no spend challenge is an effective way to help you reorganize yourself after a major event like a big wedding or after a vacation or holiday; you can also implement this after a health emergency when you had to spend a lot of money or an impulsive buying relapse.

The no spend challenge is also a great way to prepare for retirement or if you aim to go back to school or pay up a huge debt.

So, you only need to get your spreadsheets or worksheets, your pens, and get ready. Here are the rules you need to know while you are creating a no spend challenge.

Ensure you are comfortable with the no spend challenge. It is going to be a long month that seems like it will never end. I always advise people not to rush into the 30-day; you can begin with shorter periods such as the no spend weekend challenge or the no spend weekly challenge.

When you engage the no spend weekly challenge, you get involved in free activities with your family members or your friends. These activities would not require any need to spend money and it is a great way to show your kids they can live without spending.

If you engage a no spend weekly challenge, you have to opt for a lifestyle that doesn't require that you spend money on anything.

The 30-day or one month no spend challenge is more challenging than the previous 2 types because it is longer than the others. The good thing about this is that you gain more rewards from this and you can use this challenge to make better and permanent changes to your lifestyle. Psychologists say it takes 21 days to break a habit so 30 days is enough time to make the right lifestyle changes. This was how I was able to break my impulsive buying and shopping habits.

How to prepare for the 30-day no spend challenge

This challenge works when you establish some ground rules even before you begin. You can set some emergency funds aside and make sure you only spend it when there is an emergency. I always advise that keep all your debit and credit cards out of your reach. You can decide to do a bit of grocery shopping before you begin this challenge.

You are allowed to spend on other items such as rent or mortgage, insurance, health bills, utilities, important groceries, gas for your car and your phone or internet. There are activities that can make you spend more during this period and I advise that you avoid such activities. They are shopping, eating out, hanging out with friends in a bar or diner, hair, manicure, pedicure and other wants.

Now that we are clear on what we can do and what not to do, here are some other important facts that can help you to be sure that you will stay committed to this challenge throughout the 30 days.

- You need to be sure why you are getting involved in this challenge

You must have a purpose or a reason why you getting involved in this challenge before you get started. Are you doing this to get back to school so you can be eligible for a better job? Do you want to take this challenge because you want to pay off a debt? Do you want to save for your wedding or a vacation? You must have a goal for this challenge. With this knowledge in your mind, it will be easier to stay determined to your goal.

- Be sure that you can take this challenge for 30 days

If you overstretch yourself, you may not go past the first 3 days and this may discourage you from taking the challenge next time. I always advise that you don't look at this challenge as a 30-day thing; rather, see it as a daily activity. Just focus on one day at a time. You will be surprised at how quickly 30 days will pass by.

- Set rules for yourself

Write out the rules you need to follow even before you kick off this challenge. Are there things that you must buy? Are they essential? Can you live without them in one day? Are there needs you must cater for? Make this list of your needs before you start and place them in a place where you can see them daily. If they can wait till the following day then you probably don't need them.

- If you are married or you have a partner, go through the rules together

Make sure your spouse, partner or family is on the same page with you or else you wouldn't go far. Make sure everyone agrees with the ground rules for the no spend challenge so they can encourage you when you feel like quitting.

- Focus on the stock you have in your refrigerator or pantry

Instead of spending more money on groceries, focus on the stock you have in the refrigerator or pantry. Eat up these before you begin to shop for other groceries or products and you can eat up what you have before it gets expired. When you have no reason to shop for groceries, it will make you creative with the ones you have.

- Search for free entertainment suitable for the family

When you have kids, you will notice that you have to spend money always. With the 30-day no spend challenge, not spending may be a little difficult. I advise that you go online and search for activities you can carry out with your family (especially the kids) which will not require spending any money. Go online and search for free events in your neighborhood or family games you can all play together or you can all take a walk to the park.

- Keep your debit and credit cards out of sight

Make sure your cards are out of your reach to avoid falling into the spending temptation. If you keep them on you, there are higher chances that you may just buy something impulsively. It's better to have cash envelopes to curb and monitor your expenses. It will also help you to focus on the right needs so you spend money appropriately if you have to.

- Have the right attraction or distraction

Not spending money may be quite challenging and you may find out that you easily get bored. There are good ways to solve this challenge; you can get busy with chores such as gardening (if you have one) or cleaning and sorting out the house. You can arrange your room or the garage or the basement or even the pent house. It is time to get creative so de-clutter, reorganize and design the house. You can go through your stuffs and sort out the things you don't need; give it out to charity, sell it or throw it away if it isn't good enough. You can also go online and learn a hobby of your choice. There are many DIY's online so it is a good opportunity to pick up a skill.

- Curb your urge to buy something immediately

If you feel the sudden desire to buy something, don't mind that urge; if you do you will be taking steps to strengthen the impulsive buying or spending habit that you have. You can write out what you need and tell yourself that you will get it after the challenge. You will see that it is only a want and not a need.

Another way to curb this urge is to take the money you want to spend for the item and then add it to your savings. When you look at the amount of money you have saved not spent at the end of the challenge you will be impressed with yourself.

- Save your money

Create a special savings account (it can be a piggy bank) so that at the end of the challenge, you can add it to the money set out for other important stuffs such as debt repayment, going back to school, paying your rent or other plans that you have. Don't let the money go into other unimportant things.

The importance of this challenge is that you learn how to save more and spend less in such a way that you curb your spending habits. This may be pretty challenging at the beginning, but you will be impressed with yourself at the end of this challenge. You will find out that you are more focused and your mind is set on meeting your long-term goals and not on immediate gratification.

How possible is the 30-day no spend challenge?

Not spending money for 30 days seems like a really huge task but it is doable. For you to carry this out, you must first have a budget where you have written out all that you need for the month.

If you can think ahead then that's a great plus for you; this means that you can buy things that you need or things that the kids need beforehand or prepare for an upcoming event. If you know that you will be attending get together or you will be hanging out with friends, it's best you avoid this for one the period of the 30-day challenge.

The best kinds of events you can attend are the free ones where you don't need to spend any money. You can go through your mails as retailers can sometimes send messages to you about their free events.

CHAPTER SEVEN
TIPS TO HELP YOU WITH THE 30-DAY NO SPEND CHALLENGE

I wish it was so easy as to borrow a wand from Harry potter or Voldemort or the wand maker himself and then I would wave my wand and I wouldn't remember to spend any money. That's not possible! You need to understand 2 words: Stop Spending!

Some people do well with a reality check or tips to help them cut back on spending or a demotivator tool to help them deal with the spending habits.

Here is the reality check

Julia met with a family that can be described as middle-class or average with debts that they needed a big media money makeover. The first thing Julia found out was that they owed as much as $59,628 as credit-card debt. When Julia calculated this, it would take almost 2 years to be able to get rid of this debt (if they were to focus only on these bills without looking at other bills or even food, groceries or utilities.

Another thing Julia was yet to find out was that they also had a mortgage of about $250,000 to pay as well. That's almost about $310,000 which excludes daily purchases, maintenance and emergency bills. This family was not living an extravagant life, neither were they celebrities or media influencers. They were just a simple family trying to make the best of their lives which involved piling up huge financial debt.

The key to this is to understand these two keywords: STOP SPENDING!

These two words are easier said than done and I know it. For this family there were bound to swimming in the deep ocean of debt. To get them out of this debt, they would need to stop all expenses except food, utilities and the extra important groceries. This may seem not likely for some people but there is no way out of the debts but to stop spending.

It always begins with a little debt, just a few debts on the cards and then other unplanned debts and unbudgeted activities come into the picture and a few things to spend here and some wants to consider; this is how debt begin to pile up and people get into a financial mess. Financial mess will always take a toll on your mind, your health (especially mental health) and then your relationships too.

I called this the reality check because it always begins this way: debts on the cards, then you have no money to spend and then you can't borrow and the creditors need their money and you have no means to repay it. Some people become suicidal because of this.

You need to check how you spend. Do you spend more than you earn? If your answer is no and you can afford everything you have as well as living within your means then you are good. But if your answer is yes then that should be a warning signal especially if you are in debt and you aren't paying up.

So how do you put a reality check on the way you spend?

The first thing to look out for is the red light. The red light in this case is debt. Think back and determine where you incurred your debts from. Debts don't just jump on people, you walk into it. For example, if you need a car or a house, you are fully conscious when you are making that decision. If you used your cards or if you have taken loans for your debts, that is a sign for your reality check.

It's best if you plan your debt and create a budget for it; but when you have to use your credit cards to pay for your expenses and debt at the same time, that is where the challenge lies. If you do this consistently it may be too much for you.

The second thing you can do is to create a budget when you spend money on wants. There is a way to simplify your life and your finances; all you need to do is to create a special budget such as Budget Planner or other budget planning Apps to calculate the difference between what you earn and what you spend.

You really don't know what you are doing until you put it in check. Just as I was shocked the first time I tried this, you will also be shocked when you see the result. When you think you are still within budget, it shows you how far you are from it. Using the budget planner is a great way to keep you in check. You will be surprised at how much you will save in a year and you will be able to increase your savings and prioritize your budget.

However, if you aren't spending more than you earn then and you want to save up for something else then you can follow these tips

- Use the demotivator

The demotivator is a frightening but exciting tool that is meant to work with the Budget Planner so you can fully understand what it means to limit your expenses. For example, if you calculate the amount of money you spend buying coffee, sandwiches, newspapers and cigars at the end of the year, you will be shocked. The best thing you can do is to post the cost of items like this on your refrigerator or a place you can easily find it. This will demotivate you from spending so much on such items.

- Be objective when you assess your expenses

For you to be objective with yourself, you need to be as frank as a doctor dealing with a patient. Don't give excuses for the way you spend money or what you spend money on. Don't give the excuse of a festive season or a party.

Being objective means that go over what you are spending money at the end of the month. Prioritize on the important stuff and remove all the things that push you out of your budget.

When you know what is important, you need to stick to these priorities and discipline yourself to stick with it.

- Be sure of your priorities

If your income isn't large enough to cater for all your expenses, pick out what is important. Things like rent, mortgage, groceries, gas and clothing should be priority. When you make more money, then you can include more items to your budget.

FINAL NOTE
EVERY JOURNEY STARTS WITH A SINGLE STEP

Now comes the tough part. You need to take action. I know it is not easy, but if you follow the steps and tips I provided in this book I am pretty positive you will be able to reach great results!

I hope you enjoyed reading and wish you all the best on your journey. Thank you for purchasing this book. If you found it helpful feel free to share you honest review with others.

Printed in Great Britain
by Amazon

54315910R00054